Making Books with Pockets

The series of monthly activity books you've been waiting for!

Enliven every month of the year with fun, exciting learning projects that students can proudly present in a unique book format.

Each month has lessons for art, writing, reading, math, science, social studies, and poetry.

Contents

Michelle Barnett, Caitlin Rabanera, and **Ann Switzer** have taught first, second, and third grade. Their teaching experiences have involved working with limited-English-speaking students from many parts of the world, supervising student teachers, and conducting inservice sessions for colleagues. They are currently teaching in Southern California.

Congratulations on your purchase of some of the finest teaching materials in the world.

For information about other Evan-Moor products, call 1-800-777-4362 or FAX 1-800-777-4332

Visit our website http://www.evan-moor.com. Check the Product Updates link for supplements, additions, and corrections for this book.

Authors:	Michelle Barnett
	Caitlin Rabanera
	Ann Switzer
Editors:	Marilyn Evans
	Jill Norris
Copy Editor:	Cathy Harber
Illustrator:	Jo Larsen
Designer:	Cheryl Puckett
Desktop:	Shannon Frederickson

Entire contents ©1999 by EVAN-MOOR CORP.
18 Lower Ragsdale Drive, Monterey, CA 93940-5746.
Permission is hereby granted to the individual purchaser to reproduce student materials in this book for noncommercial individual or classroom use only. Permission is not granted for schoolwide, or systemwide, reproduction of materials.
Printed in U.S.A.

Evan-Moor
EDUCATIONAL PUBLISHERS
EMC 584

January's Special Days

Here are ideas for celebrating some of the other special days in January.

January 1 _____ **New Year's Day**

The American celebration of this holiday includes a ball dropping in Times Square, New York City, and the Rose Parade in Pasadena, California. Have students look up each city on a map.

Cook and eat black-eyed peas for good luck.

Second Monday _____ **Clean Off Your Desk Day**

Give the classroom a real tidying up!

January 18 _____ **A.A. Milne's Birthday**

Read a chapter from _Winnie the Pooh_.

January 23 _____ **National Pie Day**

Chant nursery rhymes about pies: "Little Jack Horner" and "Sing a Song Of Sixpence." Read _The Apple Pie Tree_ by Zoe Hall (Scholastic, 1996) or _Piggie Pie_ by Margie Palatini (Clarion Books, 1995).

Make a pie to share or bring in pies ready to eat.

January 27 _____ **Mozart's Birthday**

Play selections from _The Magic Flute_ or other Mozart pieces for your class.

January 29 _____ **Bill Peet's Birthday**

Read _Hubert's Hair Raising Adventure_ or _Big Bad Bruce_.

January

Sunday	Monday	Tuesday	Wednesday	Thursday	Friday	Saturday

Making Books with Pockets • January • EMC 584

How to Make Pocket Books

Each pocket book has a cover and three or more pockets. Choose construction paper colors that are appropriate to the theme of the book. Using several colors in a book creates an effective presentation.

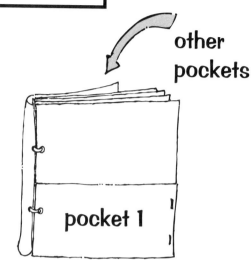

other pockets

pocket 1

Materials

- 12" x 18" (30.5 x 45.5 cm) piece of construction paper for each pocket
- cover as described for each book
- hole punch
- stapler
- string, ribbon, twine, raffia, etc., for ties

Steps to Follow

1. Fold the construction paper to create a pocket. After folding, the paper should measure 12" (30.5 cm) square.

2. Staple the right side of each pocket closed.

3. Punch two or three holes in the left side of each pocket and the cover.

4. Fasten the book together using your choice of material as ties.

5. Glue the poem or information strips onto each pocket as shown on the overview pages of each book.

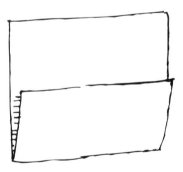

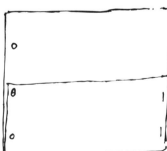

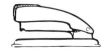

The Four Seasons

The activities in this pocket book give students an overview of all the seasons. Students will create art projects and get lots of nonfiction writing practice. What a great way to start out the new year!

The Four Seasons
Book Overview _____ **pages 6 and 7**
These pages show and tell what is in each pocket.

Cover Design _____ **pages 8 and 9**

Pocket Projects _____ **pages 10–31**
Step-by-step directions and patterns for the activities that go in each pocket.

Pocket Labels _____ **pages 32 and 33**
This poem can also be used for pocket chart activities throughout the month:
- Chant the poem
- Listen for rhyming words
- Learn new vocabulary
- Identify sight words
- Put words or lines in the correct order

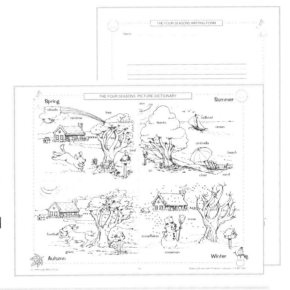

Picture Dictionary _____ **page 34**
Use the picture dictionary to introduce new vocabulary and as a spelling reference. Students can add new pictures, labels, and descriptive adjectives to the page as their vocabulary increases.

Writing Form _____ **page 35**
Use this form for story writing or as a place to record additional vocabulary words.

BIBLIOGRAPHY

Around the Pond: Who's Been Here? by Lindsay Barrett George; Greenwillow, 1996.
Circle of Seasons by Gerda Miller; Dutton Books, 1995.
It's Pumpkin Time by Zoe Hall; Scholastic, 1994.
Little Farm by the Sea by Kay Chorao; Henry Holt & Co., 1998.
Night Sounds, Morning Colors by Rosemary Wells; Dial Books for Young Readers, 1994.
The Reasons for Seasons by Gail Gibbons; Holiday House, 1995.
The Seasons of Arnold's Apple Tree by Gail Gibbons; Harcourt Brace & Co., 1984.
Spring by Ron Hirschi; Penguin Group, 1990.
Sunshine Makes the Seasons by Franklin M. Branley; Harpercollins Publishers, 1985.
When Spring Comes by Robert Maass; Henry Holt and Company, 1994.
The Year at Maple Farm by Alice and Martin Provensen; Aladdin Books, 1978.

POCKET 1

The Seasons of an Apple Tree—Winter   page 10

After reading *The Seasons of Arnold's Apple Tree* by Gail Gibbons, students will use torn paper and sponge-painting techniques to depict the tree in winter.

Winter Is...   pages 11 and 12

Students use the form provided to write about the characteristics of this season.

Torn-Paper Snowman   pages 13 and 14

Real buttons and a fabric scarf make this snowman a charming collage.

POCKET 2

The Seasons of an Apple Tree—Spring   page 15

Sponge painted green leaves and pink-and-white tissue paper blossoms create an apple tree in spring.

Spring Is...   pages 16 and 17

Students write about spring on the reproducible writing form provided.

Things That Spring Book   pages 18 and 19

Inside this kangaroo-shaped book, students write and draw things that "spring."

POCKET 3

The Seasons of an Apple Tree—Summer　　　**page 20**

The summer apple tree has lots of red apples made by dipping a pencil eraser in paint and stamping it on the tree.

Summer Is...　　　**pages 21 and 22**

Students write about summer on the reproducible writing form provided.

Summer Beach Scene　　**pages 23 and 24**

Sandpaper is used to make the beach for this textured scene.

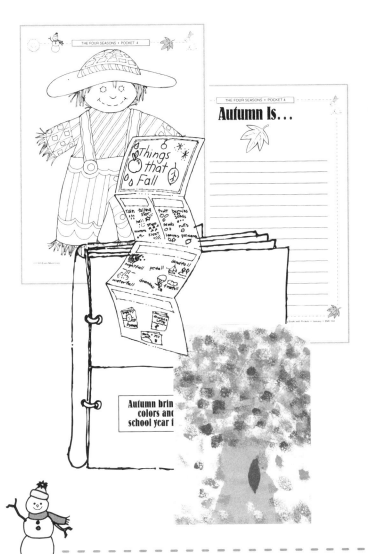

POCKET 4

The Seasons of an Apple Tree—Autumn　　　**page 25**

Sponge painted leaves of red, yellow, orange, and brown cover the tree and fall to the ground.

Autumn Is...　　　**pages 26 and 27**

After talking about autumn, students use the writing form to show what they know.

Scarecrow Crayon Resist pages 28 and 29

Color and cut out this scarecrow and then cover him with a blue watercolor wash.

Things That Fall Book　　**pages 30 and 31**

This book "falls" open to reveal pictures of things that "fall."

Materials

- construction paper

  white, 12" (30.5 cm) square
  blue, green, yellow, orange, 6" (15 cm) squares
  scraps of various colors

- patterns on page 9, reproduced
  for each student

- scissors

- glue

- crayons or marking pens

- fine-point black marker

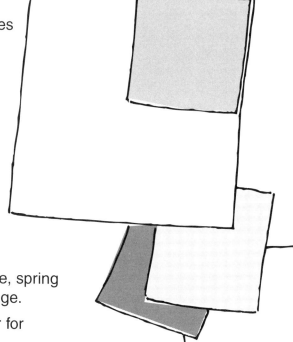

Steps to Follow

1. Color the seasonal patterns and cut them out.

2. Glue the winter pattern pieces to the blue square, spring
   to green, summer to yellow, and autumn to orange.

3. Add "extras" cut from construction paper—water for
   the sailboat, raindrops, snowflakes, etc.

4. Glue the four squares to the white paper as shown.

5. Using a black marker, write the appropriate season
   name on each square. Draw arrows to show the correct
   progression of the seasons.

Cover Patterns

The Seasons of an Apple Tree
Winter

In each of the pockets, students will follow directions to depict what an apple tree looks like during that season. Specific directions are given in the section for each pocket.

Read *The Seasons of Arnold's Apple Tree* by Gail Gibbons. Discuss how the tree changes throughout the year. On a chart or the chalkboard, write words and phrases that describe the winter apple tree.

Materials

- construction paper
  background—gray, 9" x 12" (23 x 30.5 cm)
  tree trunk—brown, 5" x 8" (13 x 20 cm)
  branches—brown scraps of various sizes
- white tempera paint
- pie tins or lids for paint containers
- small pieces of sponge
- fine-point paintbrush
- newspaper or plastic to cover painting area
- brown crayon or marking pen
- glue

Steps to Follow

1. Tear a trunk from the brown paper and glue it to the background.

2. Tear branches from scraps of brown paper and glue them to the trunk.

3. Draw a hole in the tree trunk with brown crayon or marker.

4. Sponge paint "snow" onto the top surfaces of the branches and along the bottom of the page.

5. Using the paintbrush, add snowflakes to the background.

Winter Is...

Learning about Winter

Depending on where you live, your students' understanding of winter weather may vary greatly. Provide as much information as students need—use books, films, and videos and share personal experiences. Record the information learned and shared on a chart that students may reference when they write about winter.

Be sure to discuss the following ideas to give students a variety of things to write about:

- winter weather—snow, rain, colder temperatures, blizzards
- short days and long nights
- winter recreation
- special winter clothing and transportation
- winter holidays
- the dates on which the season begins and ends

Use a globe and a sun to demonstrate how the tilt of the Earth on its axis and the revolution around the sun combine to create the seasons. Mark your location with an "X." As you move the "Earth" around the "sun," be sure to keep the North Pole pointed at the same place in the room to maintain the inclination of the Earth on its axis. Point out that winter is when your part of the Earth is pointed away from the sun.

Writing about Winter

1. Reproduce the writing form on page 12 for each student.

2. Review all the information about winter that you've written on the chart.

3. Have students write about the season. Vary the requirements of the assignment to suit the writing abilities of your students.

Winter Is...

_____

_____

_____

_____

_____

_____

_____

_____

_____

_____

_____

_____

Torn-Paper Snowman

As a symbol of winter, no matter where you live, the snowman readily captures kids' imaginations. The finishing touches that students will put on their snowmen or snowwomen make each one unique.

Materials

- construction paper
  background—dark blue, 9" x 12" (23 x 30.5 cm)
  ground—white, 4" x 9" (10 x 23 cm)
  bottom snowball—white, 5" x 7" (13 x 18 cm)
  middle snowball—white, 4" x 5" (10 x 13 cm)
  snowman's head—white, 3" x 4" (7.5 x 10 cm)
  hat—any color, 3" x 6" (7.5 x 15 cm)
  scarf—any color 4" (10 cm) square
  decorations—scraps of black, orange, and white
- tagboard templates for hat and scarf, made from patterns on page 14
- small buttons of varying colors
- glue
- scissors
- optional—fabric scraps for scarf

Steps to Follow

1. Tear a snowy hill for the ground and glue it to the bottom of the blue paper.

2. Tear the edges of the three body pieces to make roundish "snowballs."

3. Glue the snowballs (overlapping them slightly) to the background to make the snowman.

4. Use one of the hat templates to trace and cut the hat. Glue the hat to the snowman's head. Decorate the hat if desired.

5. Use the scarf template to trace and cut the scarf from any bright-colored paper. Glue the scarf to the neck of the snowman. (If your students are able to cut fabric, make the scarves from gaily printed scraps.)

6. Glue two buttons to the middle section of the snowman.

7. Use scraps of construction paper to make eyes, a nose, and arms.

8. Optional—Cut small snowflakes from white paper and glue to the background.

Snowman Templates

horizontal scarf piece

vertical scarf piece

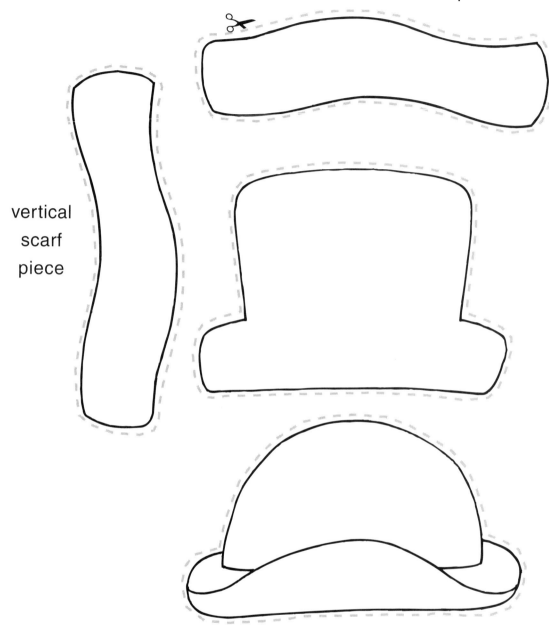

Making Books with Pockets • January • EMC 584

The Seasons of an Apple Tree
Spring

Review what students remember of *The Seasons of Arnold's Apple Tree*. Share the pictures of the tree in spring and make a list of the important features.

Materials

- construction paper
  background—light blue, 9" x 12"
  (23 x 30.5 cm)
  tree trunk—brown, 5" x 8" (13 x 20 cm)
  branches—brown scraps of various sizes
- green tempera paint
- pie tins or lids for paint containers
- small pieces of sponge
- small pieces of pink and white tissue paper
- newspaper or plastic to cover painting area
- brown crayon or marking pen
- glue

Steps to Follow

1. Tear a trunk from the brown paper and glue it to the background.

2. Tear branches from scraps of brown paper and glue them to the trunk.

3. Draw a hole in the tree trunk with brown crayon or marker.

4. Sponge paint green "leaves" onto the branches and green "grass" along the bottom of the page.

5. To make blossoms, wrap small pieces of white tissue paper around the eraser end of a pencil. Dip the tissue in glue and then affix to a tree branch. Repeat, using pink tissue paper. Put a white tissue piece and a pink tissue piece next to each other to give the effect of the two-tone apple blossoms.

Spring Is...

Learning about Spring

Spring can be a season of joyous change if you live in colder areas; or it can mean just slightly warmer temperatures and longer days if you live in a more temperate area. Provide as much information about the season as students need—use books, films, and videos and share personal experiences. Record the information learned and shared on a chart that students may reference when they write about spring.

Be sure to discuss the following ideas to give students a variety of things to write about:

- spring weather—rain, thundershowers, warmer temperatures
- days are getting longer
- new growth—flowers, trees leaf out, baby birds and animals
- colors change from gray and brown to green
- spring recreation
- spring holidays
- the dates on which the season begins and ends

Use a globe and a sun to demonstrate how the tilt of the Earth on its axis and the revolution around the sun combine to create the seasons. Mark your location with an "X." As you move the "Earth" around the "sun," be sure to keep the North Pole pointed at the same place in the room to maintain the inclination of the Earth on its axis. Point out that spring is when your part of the Earth is pointed just slightly away from the sun.

Writing about Spring

1. Reproduce the writing form on page 17 for each student.

2. Review all the information about spring that you've written on the chart.

3. Have students write about the season. Vary the requirements of the assignment to suit the writing abilities of your students.

Spring Is...

_____

_____

_____

_____

_____

_____

_____

_____

_____

_____

_____

Things That Spring Book

Presenting the Lesson

Ask students if they know another meaning for the word "spring" besides the name of a season. Elicit the response that "spring" also means to leap, jump, or hop. Brainstorm and list things that spring.

Have each student choose their favorite things that spring to write and draw in their book. Older students may want to think up new items and create an original book.

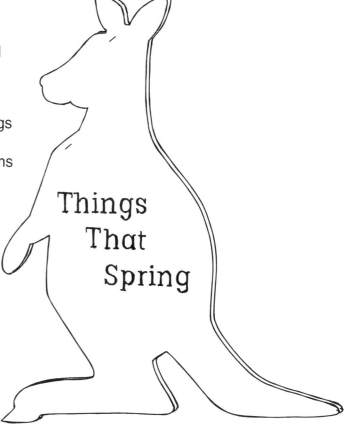

Things That Spring

Making the Book

Material

- tagboard template made from pattern on page 19
- two 8" x 10" (20 x 25.5 cm) pieces of yellow construction paper
- pattern on page 19, reproduced on copier paper—quantity determined by the number of pages that you wish to be in each student's book
- crayons
- pencil
- stapler

Steps to Follow

1. Using the tagboard template, trace and cut a front and back cover.

2. Cut out inside pages.

3. Put the inside pages between the covers and staple on the top left side between the ears and front leg.

4. Write the title "Things That Spring" on the cover.

5. On each page in the book, draw a picture of something that springs. Write the name of the picture.

Kangaroo Pattern

Making Books with Pockets • January • EMC 584

The Seasons of an Apple Tree
Summer

Review what students remember about *The Seasons of Arnold's Apple Tree*. Share the pictures of the tree in summer and make a list of the important features.

Materials

- construction paper
  background—light blue, 9" x 12" (23 x 30.5 cm)
  tree trunk—brown, 5" x 8" (13 x 20 cm)
  branches—brown scraps of various sizes
- green and red tempera paint
- pie tins or lids for paint containers
- small pieces of sponge
- pencils with erasers
- newspaper or plastic to cover painting area
- brown crayon or marking pen
- glue

Steps to Follow

1. Tear a trunk from the brown paper and glue it to the background.

2. Tear branches from scraps of brown paper and glue them to the trunk.

3. Draw a hole in the tree trunk with brown crayon or marker.

4. Sponge paint green "leaves" onto the branches and green "grass" along the bottom of the page. There should be more leaves than were on the spring tree.

5. Dip the eraser end of a pencil in the red paint and print "apples" on the tree.

Summer Is...

Learning about Summer

Who doesn't look forward to summer—the warmest season no matter where you live—the time of vacations and outdoor fun? Provide as much information about the season as students need—use books, films, and videos and share personal experiences. Record the information learned and shared on a chart that students may reference when they write about summer.

Be sure to discuss the following ideas to give students a variety of things to write about:

- summer weather—heat, thunderstorms (maybe tornadoes), long days
- things in nature are growing—flowers, fruits, and vegetables
- summer recreation
- vacation destinations
- special summer clothes
- summer holidays
- the dates on which the season begins and ends

Use a globe and a sun to demonstrate how the tilt of the Earth on its axis and the revolution around the sun combine to create the seasons. Mark your location with an "X." As you move the "Earth" around the "sun," be sure to keep the North Pole pointed at the same place in the room to maintain the inclination of the Earth on its axis. Point out that summer is when your part of the Earth is pointed toward the sun.

Writing about Summer

1. Reproduce the writing form on page 22 for each student.

2. Review all the information about summer that you've written on the chart.

3. Have students write about the season. Vary the requirements of the assignment to suit the writing abilities of your students.

Summer Is...

_____

_____

_____

_____

_____

_____

_____

_____

_____

_____

_____

Summer Beach Scene

Before making this sunny summer scene, read a story that takes place at the beach, such as:

- *At the Beach with Dad* by Gina Mayer and Mercer Mayer; Inchworm Press, 1998.
- *Beach Feet* by Lynn W. Reiser; Greenwillow, 1996.

Materials

- patterns on page 24, reproduced on white construction paper
- construction paper
  background—turquoise, 9" x 12" (23 x 30.5 cm)
  ocean—dark blue, 3½" x 12" (9 x 30.5 cm)
  sun—yellow, 3½" (9 cm) square
  scraps of yellow and brown

- 100-grain sandpaper
  2½" x 8" (6.5 x 20 cm)
  2½" x 5" (6.5 x 13 cm)
- black marker
- scissors
- marking pens or crayons
- glue

Steps to Follow

1. Tear the sun and its rays from yellow construction paper. Glue them to the upper-right corner of the background.

2. Cut "waves" in the "ocean" and glue them to the bottom of the background.

3. Cut the sandpaper into wavy sand hills. Glue to the bottom of the background on top of the water. Overlap the two pieces.

4. Color the patterns using brightly colored marking pens (or crayons).

5. Cut out the patterns and glue them in a pleasing arrangement on the background. Add a pole for the umbrella. Glue the sunglasses onto the face of the sun. Give "Old Sol" a little smile, too.

Summer Beach Scene Patterns

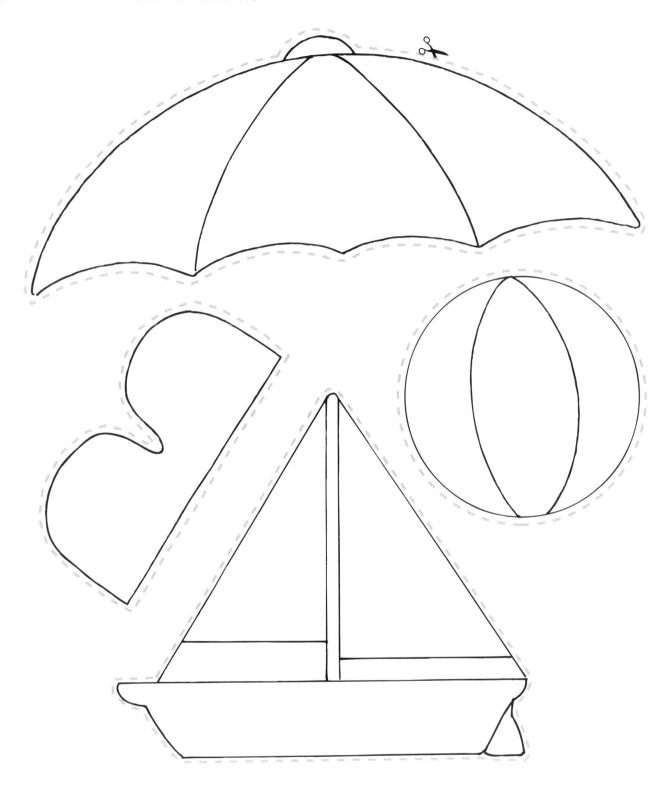

The Seasons of an Apple Tree
Autumn

Review what students remember of
The Seasons of Arnold's Apple Tree.
Share the pictures of the tree in autumn
and make a list of the important features.

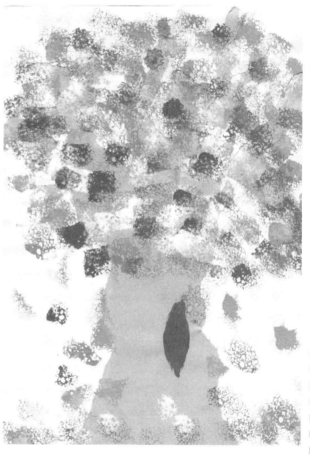

Materials

- construction paper
  background—light blue, 9" x 12" (23 x 30.5 cm)
  tree trunk—brown, 5" x 8" (13 x 20 cm)
  branches—brown scraps of various sizes
- red, yellow, orange, and brown tempera paint
- pie tins or lids for paint containers
- small pieces of sponge
- newspaper or plastic to cover painting area
- brown crayon or marking pen
- glue

Steps to Follow

1. Tear a trunk from the brown paper and glue
   it to the background.

2. Tear branches from scraps of brown paper and glue
   them to the trunk.

3. Draw a hole in the tree trunk with brown crayon or marker.

4. Sponge paint brightly colored autumn leaves on the tree
   and the ground. Be sure to show some falling, too.

Making Books with Pockets • January • EMC 584

Autumn Is...

Learning about Autumn

Like winter, autumn can be a very different experience if you live in Vermont or Ohio than it is if Arizona or Florida is your home. Provide as much information about the season as students need—use books, films, and videos and share personal experiences. Record the information learned and shared on a chart that students may reference when they write about autumn.

Be sure to discuss the following ideas to give students a variety of things to write about:

- autumn weather—cooler temperatures; maybe frost; clear, crisp days
- days are getting shorter
- a time for harvesting fruits, grains, and nuts
- back to school in many places
- autumn recreation
- autumn holidays
- the dates on which the season begins and ends

Use a globe and a sun to demonstrate how the tilt of the Earth on its axis and the revolution around the sun combine to create the seasons. Mark your location with an "X." As you move the "Earth" around the "sun," be sure to keep the North Pole pointed at the same place in the room to maintain the inclination of the Earth on its axis. Point out that autumn is when your part of the Earth is pointed just slightly away from the sun. (Some students may notice the similarity between the angle of inclination in spring and summer. You may want to point out that on the first day of both spring and fall, there are an equal number of hours of daylight and darkness.)

Writing about Autumn

1. Reproduce the writing form on page 27 for each student.

2. Review all the information about autumn that you've written on the chart.

3. Have students write about the season. Vary the requirements of the assignment to suit the writing abilities of your students.

Autumn Is...

_____

_____

_____

_____

_____

_____

_____

_____

_____

_____

_____

Making Books with Pockets • January • EMC 584

Scarecrow Crayon Resist

As a lead-in to this charming art project, read *The Little Scarecrow Boy*, an old story by Margaret Wise Brown with terrific new illustrations by Caldecott winner David Diaz (HarperCollins, 1998), or *Scarecrow* by Cynthia Rylant (Harcourt Brace, 1998.)

Demonstrate the crayon-resist technique for students. Show them how coloring heavily is more effective.

Materials

- scarecrow pattern on page 29, reproduced on white construction paper
- crayons
- folded newspaper to color on
- newspaper or plastic to cover the painting surface
- watercolors
- watercolor brushes
- containers of water
- optional—scraps of green and yellow construction paper

Steps to Follow

1. Have students creatively color the scarecrow. (If you place the pattern on a folded section of newspaper, it is much easier for students to color heavily.)

2. Students paint over the entire page with a blue watercolor wash.

3. If desired, when the paint is dry, add details with cut and/or torn paper—cornstalks, a harvest moon, etc.

Things That Fall Book

Presenting the Lesson

In some places the word "fall" is used synonymously with autumn. Use a word web to brainstorm and list "things that fall."

Make a word web on chart paper. Label the title of the web and the four main points as follows:

Things that fall from the sky
rain, sleet, meteors, falling star, snow, hail

Stories & Rhymes that fall
Humpty Dumpty, Jack and Jill, Chicken Little, London Bridge, Ring Around the Rosies

Things That Fall

Things that fall from trees
fruit, seeds, leaves, nuts, pinecones, baby birds

Words with "fall" in them
nightfall, waterfall, pitfall, downfall, freefall, landfall

Making the Book

Materials

- 8" x 24" (20 x 61 cm) white butcher paper
- pattern on page 31, reproduced for each student
- crayons
- glue
- black marking pen
- pencil

Steps to Follow

1. Accordion-fold the paper in fourths lengthwise.

2. Color and cut out the title. Glue it to the top section, making sure the fold is on the bottom.

3. With the marking pen, divide the second section in two. Cut out the labels "things that fall from the sky" and "things that fall from the trees." Glue one label in each section.

4. Cut out the remaining labels and glue them in the next two sections.

5. Draw and label pictures in each section of the book.

6. Hold the books by the top edge and let them "fall" open!

Things that fall from the sky:

Things that fall from the trees:

Words with fall:

Stories that fall:

Note: Reproduce this page and page 33 to label each of the four pockets of the Four Seasons book.

Pocket 1

Winter brings snow and rain, and icicles that freeze.

Pocket 2

Spring brings flowers, baby birds, and a gentle breeze.

Pocket 3

Summer brings vacations and hot days in the sun.

Pocket 4

Autumn brings changing colors and a new school year full of fun.

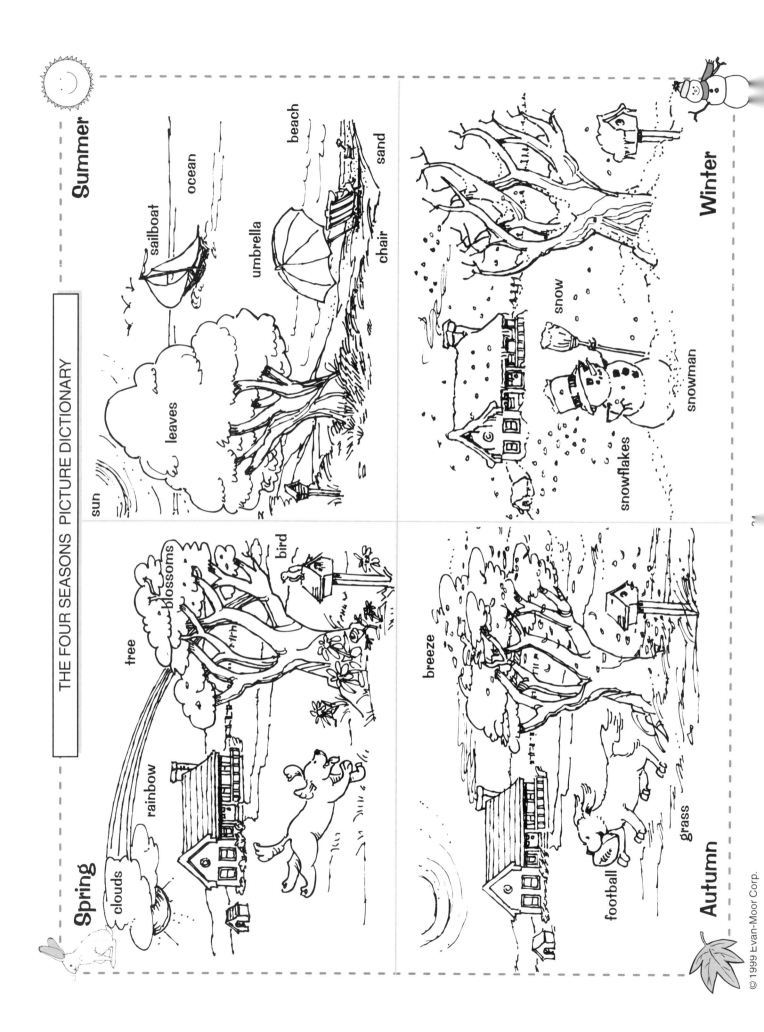

THE FOUR SEASONS PICTURE DICTIONARY

Spring

clouds
rainbow
tree
blossoms
bird

Summer

sun
sailboat
ocean
beach
sand
umbrella
chair
leaves

Winter

snow
snowman
snowflakes

Autumn

breeze
football
grass

Name: _____

Penguins

Penguins are "cool"! Your students will love studying these unusual birds of the Southern Hemisphere. While students are engaged in recording factual information, creating original stories, and making creative art projects, they will learn about types of penguins and where and how they live. As a bonus, students will gain an appreciation of the fragile environment found on the Earth's southernmost continent, Antarctica.

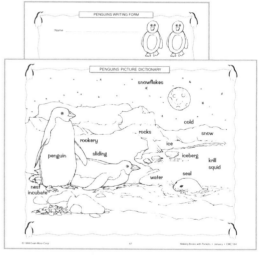

BIBLIOGRAPHY

Birds of Antarctica—The Adélie Penguin by Jennifer Owings Dewey; Little, Brown, 1989.
Little Penguin by Patrick Benson; Pholomel Books, 1990.
Looking at Penguins by Dorothy Hinshaw Patent; Holiday House, 1993.
Penguin by Caroline Arnold; Morrow Junior Books, 1988.
The Penguin: A Funny Bird by Beatrice Fontanel; Charlesbridge, 1989.
The Penguin Family Book by Laurity Somme; Picture Book Studio, 1988.
Penguins by Annette Barkhausen and Franz Geiser; Gareth Stevens, 1994.
Penguins by Sylvia A. Johnson; Lerner Publications Company, 1981.
Penguins at Home: Gentoos of Antarctica by Bruce McMillan; Houghton Mifflin, 1993.
Penguins of the World by Wayne Lynch; Firefly Books, 1997.
The Penguin's Tale by Audrey Wood; Scholastic, 1989.
Playing with Penguins by Ann McGovern; Scholastic, 1987.

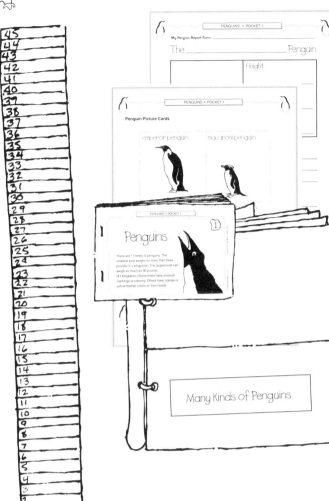

POCKET 1

Penguins Minibook   pages 42–45

Students cut apart and staple these pages together to make a book of basic information about penguins.

Penguins Picture Cards and Report Form   pages 46–48

Use the picture cards and the report form to research and find out about 8 of the 17 types of penguins.

How Tall Is a Penguin?   pages 49–51

Research the heights of different kinds of penguins and record them on either an inch or a centimeter measurement device.

POCKET 2

Where Do Penguins Live?   pages 52–54

Students cut out pictures of penguins and glue them on a map to show where they live.

Where the Penguins Live Flap Book   pages 55 and 56

A cute penguin with 3-D wings adorns this creative writing project.

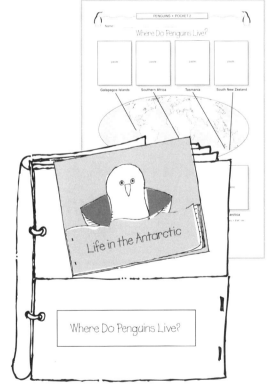

Survival   pages 57 and 58

Read about what penguins eat and what poses a threat to penguins. Then cut and paste pictures to show dangers to penguins and food for penguins.

Where Penguins
Lay Their Eggs   pages 59–62

Four little stories tell the nesting habits of four types of penguins. Students cut these out and make a double-hinged book.

Emperor Penguin
Life Cycle Wheel   pages 63–65

Students cut out pictures of the emperor penguin's life cycle, paste them to a wheel, and write about each part of the life cycle. Turn the wheel cover to see one step of the life cycle at a time.

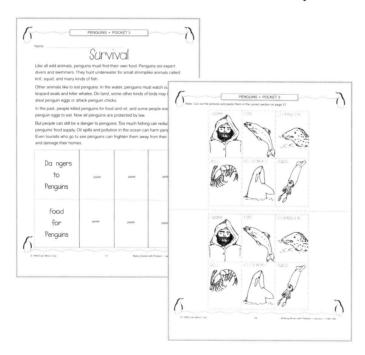

Materials

- construction paper
  cover & body—black, 12" x 18" (30.5 x 45.5 cm)
  stomach—white, 9" x 12" (23 x 30.5 cm)
  eyes—white, 3" x 4" (7.5 x 10 cm)
       black, 2" (5 cm) square

- patterns on page 40, reproduced on
  orange construction paper

- glue

- scissors

Steps to Follow

1. Round top of large black paper
   to make the penguin's head.

2. Tear the large white paper into an oval
   for the penguin's stomach. Glue this
   to the middle of the body.

3. Cut out the feet and beak.

4. Glue the feet to the backside of the penguin's
   body at the bottom. Glue the beak just above
   the white stomach.

5. Fold the black and the white eye pieces in half.
   Round all the corners to make inner and outer parts of the eyes.

6. Glue the eye parts together and glue them just above the beak.

Penguin Feet and Beak Patterns

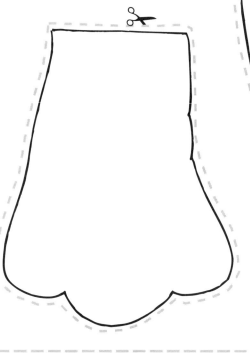

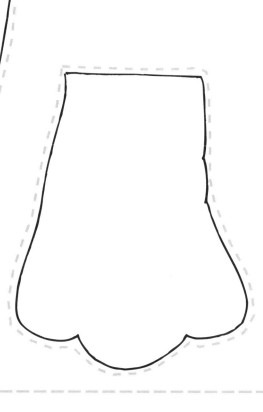

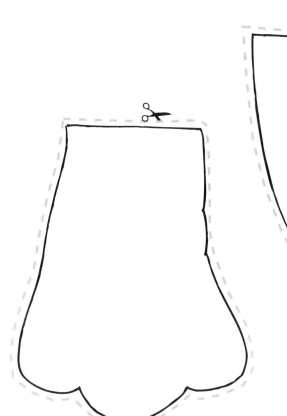

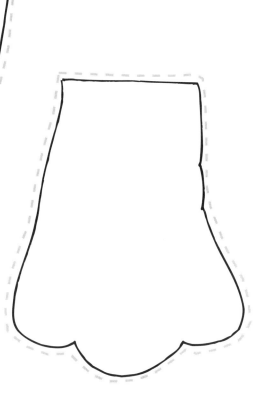

Learning about Penguins

The amount of information on penguins that you present to your class will depend on the time you've allotted for this pocket book and the interest and ability levels of your students.

Some factual information is provided in this unit. Augment this with books listed in the bibliography on page 36 and other current resources that you locate. There are a number of terrific penguin sites on the World Wide Web. As sites do change, none are listed here. Use the key words "penguins, bird" and search on Yahooligans for some good links.

Penguins Minibook

Some basic information about penguins is provided in the minibook on pages 42–45. Have students cut the pages apart and staple them together and then put the book in the first pocket of their penguin books.

Penguin Picture Cards and Report Form

The picture cards on pages 46 and 47 show 8 of the 17 types of penguins. Read about these kinds of penguins in your classroom resources* or on the WWW, complete the report form on page 48 for each penguin, and attach the illustration. Depending on the level of your students, you may want to do this as a whole class, in small groups, or independently.

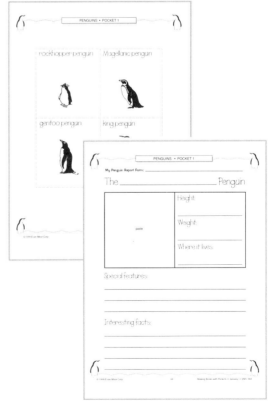

Penguins by Annette Barkhausen and Franz Geiser has a section for each of the 17 types of penguins.

Penguins

1

There are 17 kinds of penguins. The smallest kind weighs no more than three pounds (1½ kilograms). The largest kind can weigh as much as 90 pounds (41 kilograms.) Some kinds have unusual markings or coloring. Others have orange or yellow feather crests on their heads.

January Pocket Book • EMC 584

2

All penguins are alike in some ways.

short neck ——

heavy body ——

—— white belly

black or blue-gray back ——

—— short, stiff wings

—— webbed feet

wedge-shaped tail ——

legs far back on body

January Pocket Book • EMC 584

3

Penguins can't fly, but they are graceful, swift swimmers. Their flat wings are powerful flippers that move them through the water.

4

Penguins' feathers are different from those of other birds. Penguin feathers are small and tightly packed together. There can be as many as 70 feathers in a square inch! The feathers overlap and are three or four layers thick. Fluffy down underneath the feathers helps hold warm air next to the penguin's skin.

All penguins are pretty much the same color. Their backs are black or blue-gray. Their bellies are white. This makes it hard for predators such as killer whales and seals to see them in the water.

Penguins gather in large groups, called rookeries, to nest and raise their babies. Penguins lay one or two eggs. After the eggs are laid, one parent goes to sea to feed. The other parent stays with the eggs until they hatch.

January Pocket Book • EMC 584

Thick, fluffy, gray or brown down covers the chicks. It will be seven or eight weeks before they begin to get their first feathers.

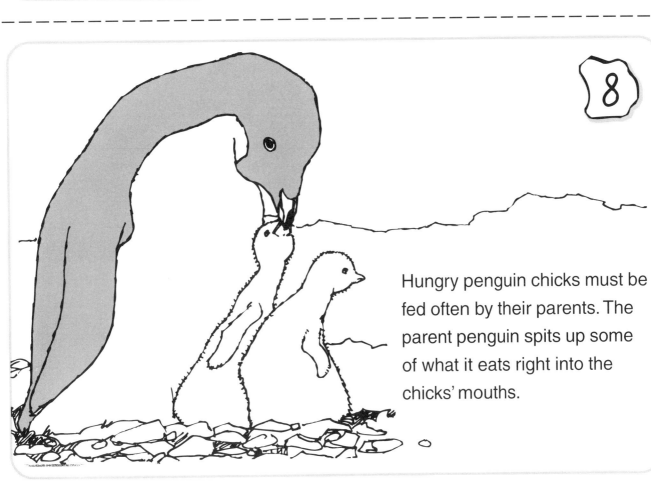

January Pocket Book • EMC 584

Hungry penguin chicks must be fed often by their parents. The parent penguin spits up some of what it eats right into the chicks' mouths.

Penguin Picture Cards

emperor penguin

macaroni penguin

little blue penguin

chinstrap penguin

Making Books with Pockets • January • EMC 584

rockhopper penguin

Magellanic penguin

gentoo penguin

king penguin

My Penguin Report Form: _____

The _____ Penguin

	Height:
	_____
paste	Weight:
	_____
	Where it lives:
	_____

Special features:

_____

_____

_____

Interesting facts:

_____

_____

_____

How Tall Is a Penguin?

Penguin	Inches	Centimeters	Penguin	Inches	Centimeters
Adélie	27	70	little blue (or fairy)	16	40
African	28	72	macaroni	28	72
chinstrap	27	70	Magellanic	28	72
erect-crested	26	66	Peruvian (Humboldt)	26	66
emperor	45	115	royal	25	64
Fiordland crested	24	60	rockhopper	22	56
Galápagos	21	54	Snares crested	22	56
gentoo	30	76	yellow-eyed	26	66
king	37	94			

Make a chart that lists all 17 kinds of penguins. As you read the information telling the height of a penguin, record it on the chart. When you have recorded as many penguins as you would like, do the size comparison project below.

Materials

- pattern on page 50 or page 51, reproduced on white construction paper—3 per student (page 50 is for U.S. Customary; page 51 is for metric)
- black marking pen
- scissors
- glue
- pencil
- crayons

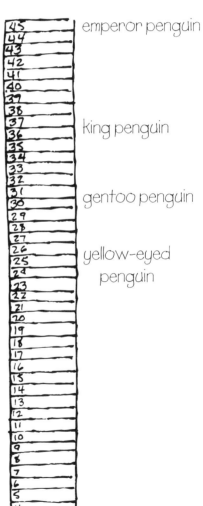

Steps to Follow

1. Cut apart each of the six sections and glue them together.

2. Starting from the bottom, number the chart on the left-hand side, using a marking pen:
   U.S. Customary is in inches; number from 1–48
   Metric is in 2-centimeter increments; number by 2's to 120

3. Write the name of the penguin in the section that tells its height. You may choose to draw a picture or symbol for each penguin, for example: a yellow eye for the yellow-eyed penguin; a crown for the emperor penguin.

4. Measure each student and mark his or her height as well.

     Making Books with Pockets • January • EMC 584

U.S. Customary

glue

glue

Metric

glue

glue

Name: _____

Where Do Penguins Live?

When you think of penguins, do you think of the icy, cold South Pole? Most people do.

Penguins do live south of the equator, in the Southern Hemisphere. But you may be surprised to learn that only two kinds of penguins live on the continent of Antarctica. The rest live in warmer places. Some live as far north as the equator.

Here is where some kinds of penguins live:

- rockhopper .... Tierra del Fuego

- little blue .... Tasmania

- Fiordland crested .... southern coast of New Zealand

- Galápagos .... Galápagos Islands

- African .... coast of southern Africa

- emperor .... Antarctica

- king .... Falkland Islands

- Adélie .... Antarctica

Cut out the 8 penguin pictures. Glue them in the correct boxes on the map page to show where they live.

Name: _____

Where Do Penguins Live?

paste	paste	paste	paste
Galapágos Islands	**Southern Africa**	**Tasmania**	**South New Zealand**

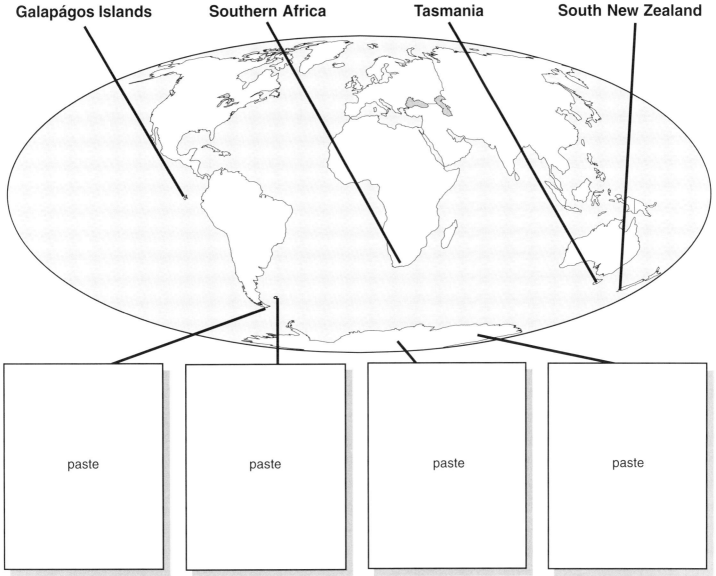

paste	paste	paste	paste
Tierra del Fuego	**Falkland Islands**	**Antarctica**	**Antarctica**

Penguin Picture Cards

emperor

king

rockhopper

little blue

African

Fiordland crested

Galápagos

Adélie

emperor

king

rockhopper

little blue

African

Fiordland crested

Galápagos

Adélie

Where the Penguins Live
A Flap Book

When you have shared sufficient information about where penguins live, have students write about what they know. You may want to give students the choice of writing factual information or basing a creative story on what they have learned. Some suggested titles are:

A Day in the Life of a Penguin

My Journey to the Penguins

Life in the Antarctic

Materials

- penguin pattern on page 56
- writing paper cut to
  4½" x 11" (11 x 28 cm)—
  several for each student
- construction paper
  back cover—blue, 9" x 12" (23 x 30.5 cm)
  front cover—blue, 4½" x 12" (11 x 30.5 cm)

- scissors
- crayons or marking pens
- glue
- stapler

Steps to Follow

1. Color and cut out the penguin.

2. Put glue on the back of the penguin but not on the wings. Glue the penguin to the large blue paper, with the head close to the top edge.

3. Cut the other sheet of blue paper in a wavy line to resemble water.

4. Have students write their stories.

5. Staple the stories and the wavy front cover to the back cover.

6. Write a title on the front cover.

7. Fold the penguin's wings down over the front cover.

Penguin Pattern

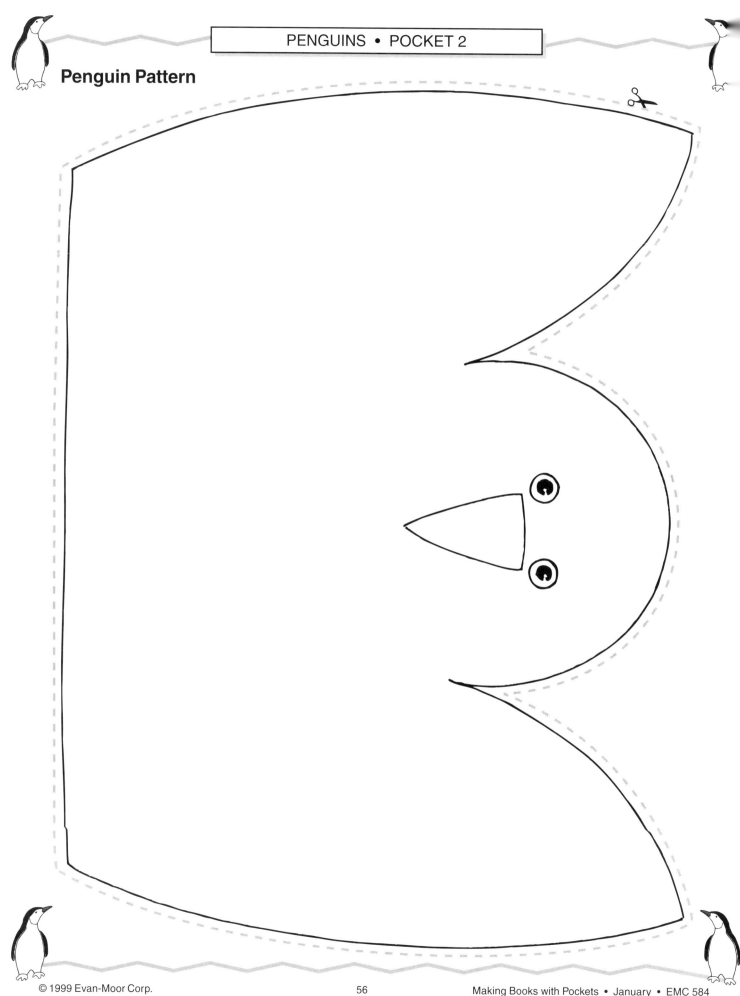

Name: _____

Survival

Like all wild animals, penguins must find their own food. Penguins are expert divers and swimmers. They hunt underwater for small shrimplike animals called krill, squid, and many kinds of fish.

Other animals like to eat penguins. In the water, penguins must watch out for leopard seals and killer whales. On land, some other kinds of birds may try to steal penguin eggs or attack penguin chicks.

In the past, people killed penguins for food and oil, and some people even took penguin eggs to eat. Now all penguins are protected by law.

But people can still be a danger to penguins. Too much fishing can reduce the penguins' food supply. Oil spills and pollution in the ocean can harm penguins. Even tourists who go to see penguins can frighten them away from their chicks and damage their homes.

Dangers to Penguins	paste	paste	paste
Food for Penguins	paste	paste	paste

Note: Cut out the pictures and paste them in the correct section on page 57.

HUMAN

FISH

LEOPARD SEAL

KRILL

KILLER WHALE

SQUID

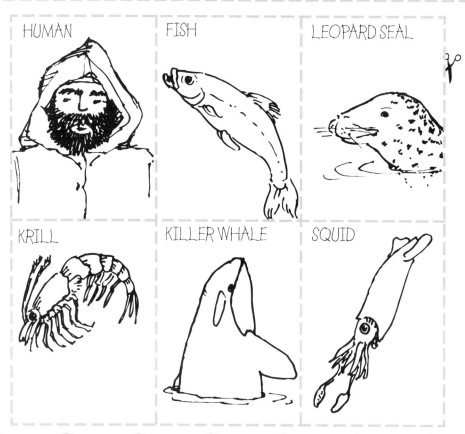

HUMAN

FISH

LEOPARD SEAL

KRILL

KILLER WHALE

SQUID

Making Books with Pockets • January • EMC 584

Where Penguins Lay Their Eggs
A Double-Hinged Book

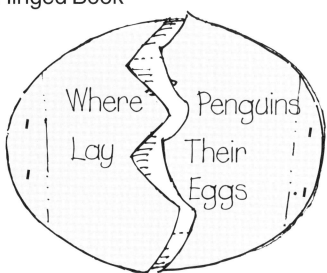

Materials

- egg cover pattern on page 60, reproduced on white or tan construction paper
- 9" x 12" (23 x 30.5 cm) piece of white or tan construction paper for back cover
- penguin information on pages 61 and 62, reproduced for each student
- scissors
- stapler

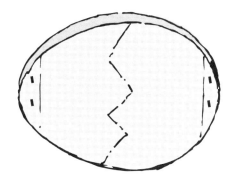

Steps to Follow

1. Read the information on pages 61 and 62 together. You many want to make an overhead transparency to use for this part of the lesson. Ask students to speculate about the reasons for such diverse egg-laying sites. Guide them to understand that the birds use what their habitats provide.

2. Students cut out the egg cover and then use it as a template to cut the back cover.

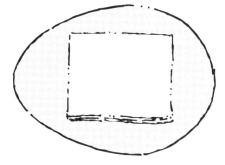

3. Students cut out the information sections and attach them to the back cover by stapling through the top edges in two places.

4. Cut the cover along the crack.

5. Staple each side of the front cover to the back cover.

6. Write the title "Where Penguins Lay Their Eggs." on the cover.

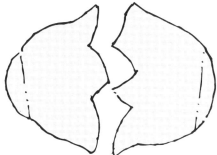

Egg Cover Pattern

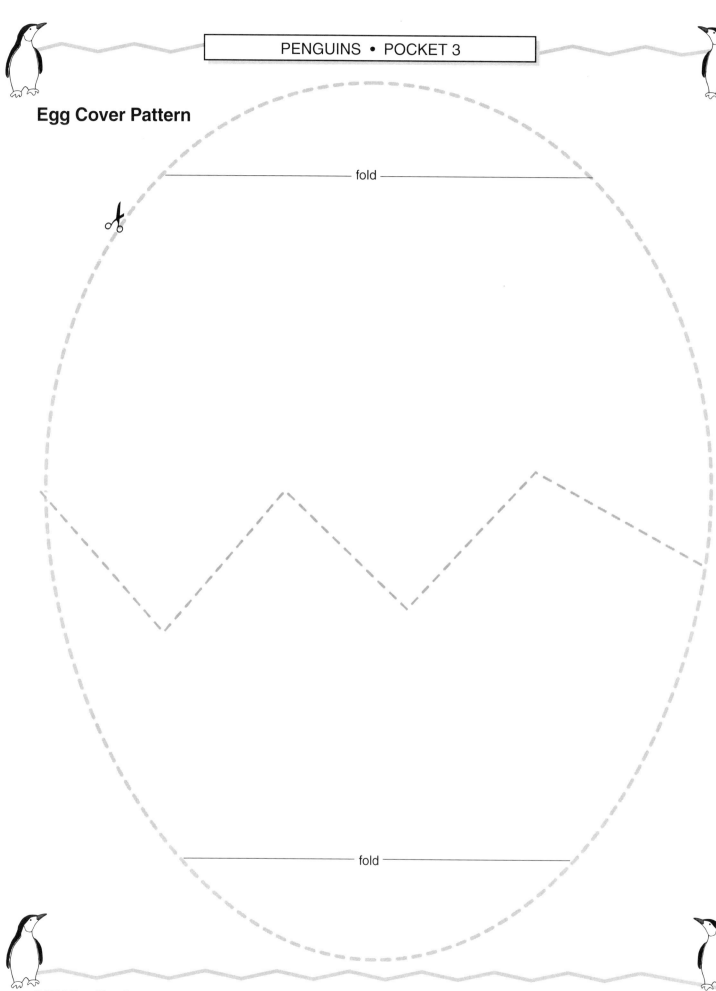

fold

fold

Adélie Penguin

Each pair of Adélie penguins has a tiny place in the rookery. In this two-foot (60 centimeter) space, the penguins build a round nest using pebbles. Sometimes they steal pebbles from their neighbors.

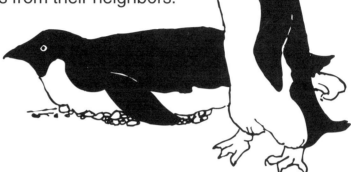

Magellanic Penguin

Magellanic penguins use their feet and beaks to dig a burrow in the ground. The burrows can be as long as 6 feet (almost 2 meters). At the end of the burrow, they mound up dried leaves, grass, sticks, and pebbles. The female lays one or two eggs in this nest.

Making Books with Pockets • January • EMC 584

Rockhopper Penguin

Rockhopper penguins nest on steep slopes. The female makes a dent in the ground. The male gathers things to make the nest. They use sticks, grass, leaves, pebbles, and even bones. The female lays two eggs. The first egg laid is much smaller and usually does not hatch.

Emperor Penguin

Emperor penguins live on the Antarctic ice. They do not build nests. The female emperor lays one egg. Then she passes the egg from her feet to the feet of her mate. He tucks the egg up into his brood pouch. This is a place on his stomach with a flap of skin over it.

Emperor Penguin Life Cycle Wheel

Read about the emperor penguins in any of the resources you have available. Both you and your students will find the story of how the male emperors incubate the eggs a fascinating one.

After discussing what they have learned, students will make a life cycle wheel to put in pocket 3 of their penguin books.

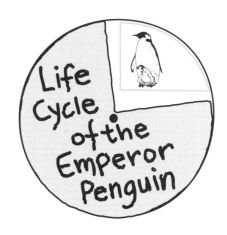

Materials

- life cycle wheel pattern on page 64, reproduced on white construction paper
- emperor penguin life cycle pictures on page 65, reproduced for each student
- 9" x 12" (23 x 30.5 cm) piece of light blue construction paper
- paper fastener
- scissors
- glue

Steps to Follow

1. Cut out the circle pattern.

2. Use the circle pattern as a template to cut a circle from the light blue construction paper.

3. Fold the blue circle in fourths, open it, and cut out most of one fourth as shown. Write "Life Cycle of the Emperor Penguin" on the blue circle.

4. Cut out the emperor penguin pictures and glue them in order, one in each section of the circle pattern.

5. On the lines, write a sentence about each picture.

6. Attach the two circles together by pushing the paper fastener through the centers.

7. Have students turn their wheels and explain the emperor penguin life cycle to a partner.

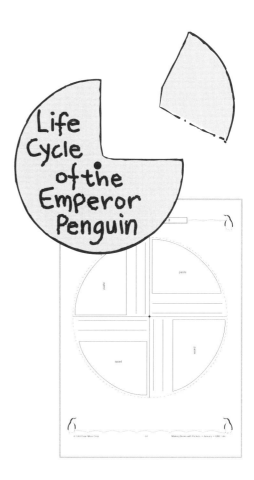

Life Cycle Wheel Pattern

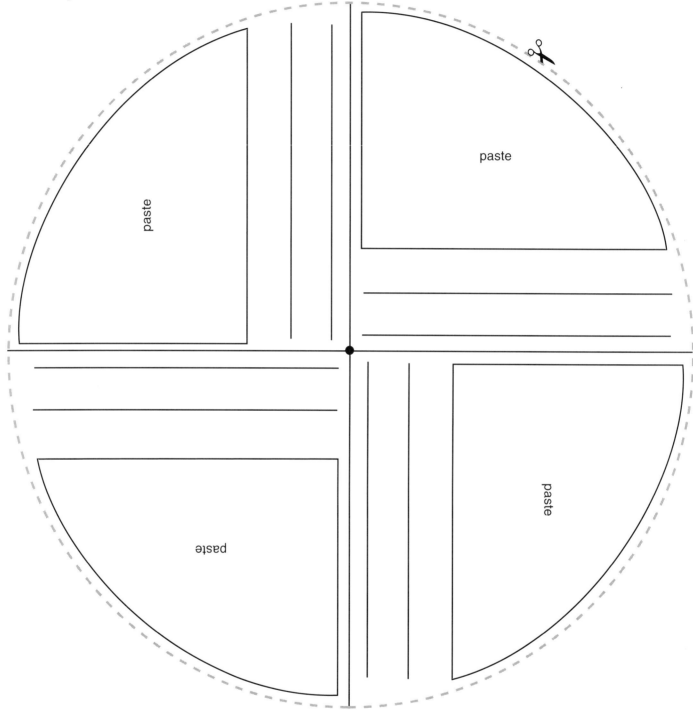

paste

paste

paste

paste

Emperor Penguin
Life Cycle Pictures

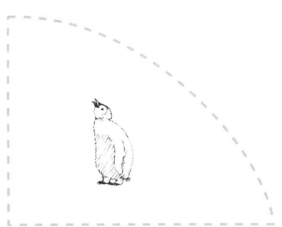

Emperor Penguin
Life Cycle Pictures

Note: Reproduce this page to label each of the three pockets in the Penguins book.

Pocket 1

Many Kinds of Penguins

Pocket 2

Where Do Penguins Live?

Pocket 3

Penguin Lifestyles

snowflakes

cold

snow

krill

squid

iceberg

ice

seal

rocks

water

sliding

rookery

penguin

nest
incubate

Making Books with Pockets • January • EMC 584

PENGUINS WRITING FORM

Name: _____

_____
- -
_____
_____
- -
_____
_____
- -
_____
_____
- -
_____
_____
- -
_____
_____
- -
_____
_____
- -
_____
_____
- -
_____
_____
- -

Famous Americans

This pocket book features four Americans born in the month of January—John Hancock, Betsy Ross, Benjamin Franklin, and Dr. Martin Luther King, Jr. As your students learn about the lives and contributions of these four Americans, they will create books, art projects, and practice critical problem solving.

Famous Americans

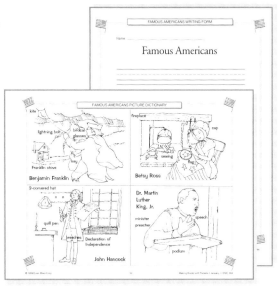

BIBLIOGRAPHY

Ben and Me... by Robert Lawson; Little, Brown, 1988.
Betsy Ross by Alexander Wallner; Holiday House, 1994.
Betsy Ross: Designer of Our Flag by Ann Weil; Aladdin Paperbacks, 1986.
Happy Birthday, Martin Luther King by Jean Marzollo; Scholastic, 1993.
Martin Luther King, Jr.—A Biography for Young Children by Carol Hilgartner; Gryphon House, 1990.
My Dream of Martin Luther King by Faith Ringgold; Crown Publishers, Inc., 1995.
A Picture Book of Benjamin Franklin by David A. Adler; Holiday House, 1990.

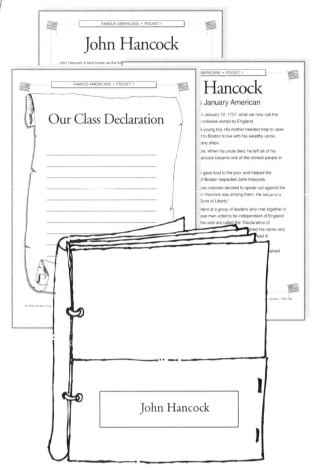

The following books are too sophisticated for most primary students. Select sections to share or use as a teacher resource.
Betsy Ross: Patriot of Philadelphia by Judith St. George; Henry Holt, 1997.
John Hancock: A Signature Life by Philip Koslow; Franklin Watts, 1998.
What's the Big Idea, Ben Franklin? by Jean Fritz; Putnam, 1976.
Will You Sign Here, John Hancock? by Jean Fritz; Coward, McCann & Geoghegan, Inc., 1976.

POCKET 1

John Hancock   **pages 76 and 77**

Students learn about this "founding father" from classroom resources, including a short biography provided.

Our Class Declaration   **page 78**

After talking about the Declaration of Independence, students write a declaration that has to do with their own lives.

POCKET 2

Betsy Ross   **page 79**

This information sheet on Betsy Ross's life can be reproduced for each student's pocketbook.

Sew a Bookmark   **page 80**

Give students an opportunity to practice sewing as they make an initialed bookmark.

**The Original
American Flag**   **pages 81 and 82**

Make a 13-star flag from construction paper and learn about what the symbols on the flag stand for.

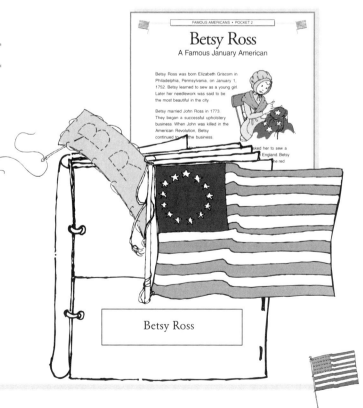

Note: Biographical information is provided for John Hancock and Betsy Ross but not provided for Benjamin Franklin or Dr. Martin Luther King, Jr., as resources on these men are easy to locate.

POCKET 3

Poor Richard's Almanac   pages 83–85

Extend what was learned about Franklin's famous book by creating individual almanacs.

Ben Franklin's Contributions   pages 86 and 87

Make a kite on which to place symbols that show just a few of this talented individual's accomplishments.

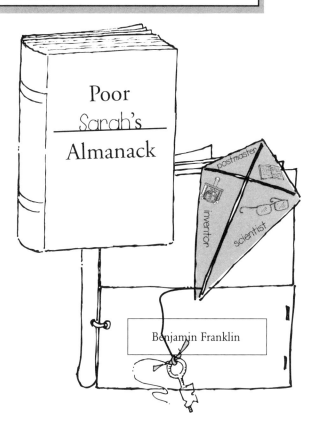

POCKET 4

Write about Dr. Martin Luther King, Jr.   pages 88 and 89

On the illustrated form provided, students write what they have learned about Dr. King.

I Can Help   page 90

The cover of this book shows two joined hands. Students write about what they can do to help realize Dr. Martin Luther King, Jr.'s dream.

You may want to make this cover after students have completed the pockets for this book so that they have a sense of the personalities and the times in which the four famous Americans lived.

Materials

- 12" (30.5 cm) square of white construction paper
- patterns on pages 73–75, reproduced on white construction paper
- marking pens or crayons
- scissors
- glue

Steps to Follow

1. Color and cut out the figures of "John" and "Martin."

2. Color and cut out the head and body pieces of "Betsy" and "Benjamin." Glue the heads to the matching body parts.

3. Lay the four figures on the white cover to establish correct placement. Glue each one in place.

4. Write "Famous Americans" across the top with a red marking pen.

5. Add decorative patterns in the open space.

John Hancock Pattern

Dr. Martin Luther King, Jr. Pattern

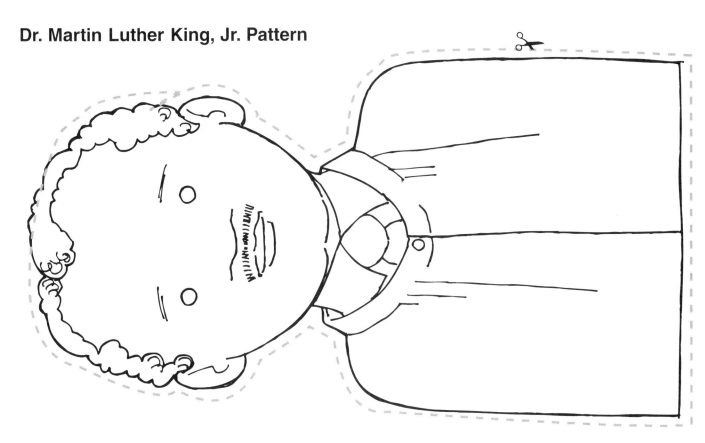

Betsy Ross Pattern

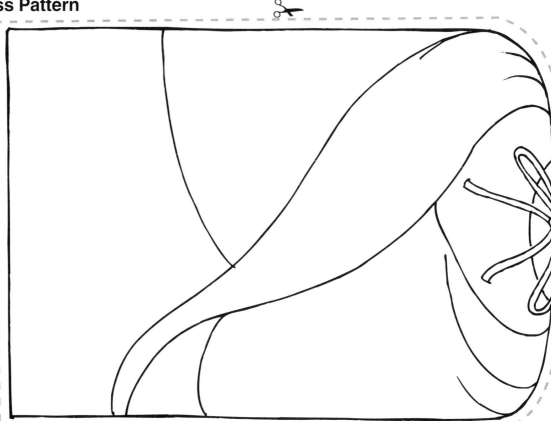

Benjamin Franklin Pattern

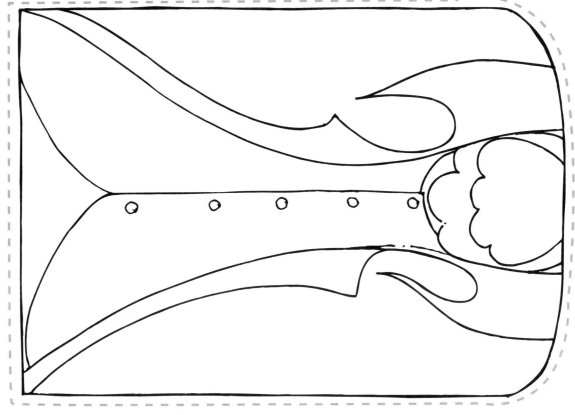

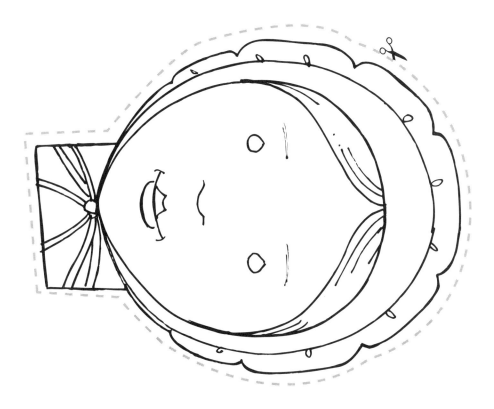

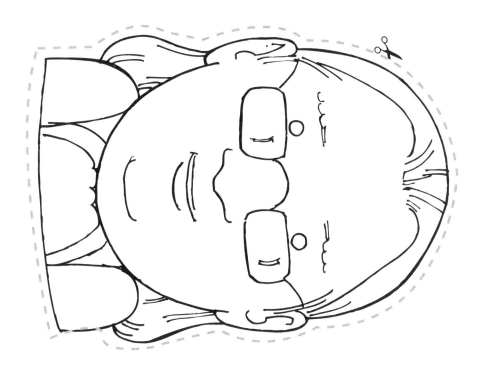

John Hancock

John Hancock is best known as the first and most flamboyant signer of the Declaration of Independence. Even today we use the expression, "Put your John Hancock here."

- Read portions of Jean Fritz's book, *Will You Sign Here, John Hancock?* or *John Hancock: A Signature Life* by Philip Koslow. Or relate the information as appropriate to your class.

  Page 77 can be reproduced for each student, read together, and added to each student's pocket.

- If possible, obtain a replica of the Declaration of Independence to share with the class. Even though they may not understand the meaning, they may appreciate the power and rhythm of the words. Discuss the document to the degree that you feel appropriate.

Discuss with your students the meaning of declaration—a formal announcement, and, in the case of the Declaration of Independence, an announcement of belief. The form on page 78 can be used to write a class declaration. This could be about students' rights as individuals in general or about how they want to be treated in the classroom and at school.

Make an overhead transparency of the form to use as you guide the class to compose its declaration. Reproduce the form so that each student can copy the completed declaration for his or her pocket book. Make the declaration extra special by reproducing it on parchment paper.

John Hancock
A Famous January American

When John Hancock was born on January 12, 1737, what we now call the United States of America was 13 colonies owned by England.

John's father died when he was a young boy. His mother needed help to raise her three children. John was sent to Boston to live with his wealthy uncle, Thomas Hancock, who owned many ships.

John was sent to the finest schools. When his uncle died, he left all of his ships to John. At age 27, John Hancock became one of the richest people in Boston.

John was a generous person. He gave food to the poor and helped the churches in the city. The people of Boston respected John Hancock.

When some people in the American colonies decided to speak out against the taxes being paid to England, John Hancock was among them. He became a part of the group known as the "Sons of Liberty."

John Hancock was elected president of a group of leaders who met together in Philadelphia. On July 4, 1776, these men voted to be independent of England. The words they used to explain this vote are called the "Declaration of Independence." John Hancock was the first to sign it. He signed his name very large so that the king of England wouldn't need his glasses to read it!

After the American colonies won their independence, the people of Massachusetts chose John Hancock to be their first governor. He remained governor until he died in 1793.

Here is what his famous signature looks like:

Our Class Declaration

Betsy Ross
A Famous January American

Betsy Ross was born Elizabeth Griscom in Philadelphia, Pennsylvania, on January 1, 1752. Betsy learned to sew as a young girl. Later her needlework was said to be the most beautiful in the city.

Betsy married John Ross in 1773. They began a successful upholstery business. When John was killed in the American Revolution, Betsy continued to run the business.

General George Washington called on Betsy and asked her to sew a flag for the colonies to symbolize their independence from England. Betsy suggested a five-pointed star for each colony on a field of blue. The red and white stripes also stand for the 13 original colonies.

Betsy Ross was married and widowed two more times. She had six children. She continued to run the upholstery business and taught her daughters and granddaughters how to sew.

Betsy Ross died in 1836. In 1870 her grandson wrote about her and her contributions to American history.

Sew a Bookmark

Betsy Ross was an accomplished seamstress. Give your students a taste of sewing by creating a useful bookmark.

Depending on the age and abilities of your students, you may want to do this project in small groups with an adult helper to thread the needles and tie the knots.

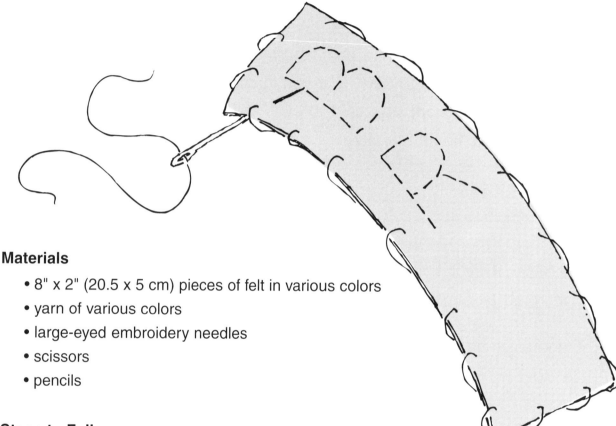

Materials

- 8" x 2" (20.5 x 5 cm) pieces of felt in various colors
- yarn of various colors
- large-eyed embroidery needles
- scissors
- pencils

Steps to Follow

1. Demonstrate how to do a blanket stitch around the edge of something. If you need to demonstrate to the whole class at once, sew around the edge of an overhead transparency so that students can follow what you are doing on the screen.

2. Have each student choose a piece of felt and a contrasting color of yarn. Assist students in doing the blanket stitch around the felt.

3. Finish off the stitched border by tying a knot in the yarn and cutting the loose end.

4. Demonstrate how to do a running stitch.

5. Have students use a pencil to lightly write their initials on the felt.

6. Stitch over the letters using the running stitch.

The Original American Flag

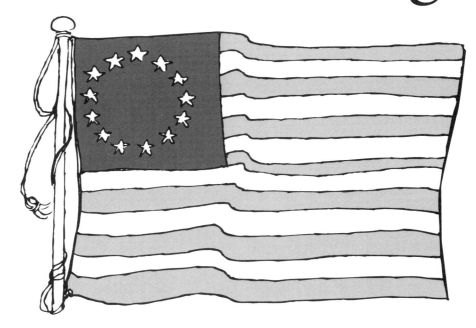

The original flag had two representations of the 13 colonies—13 stars and 13 stripes. As the country grew, there was an attempt to increase both with each new state. It soon became obvious that it wouldn't work to keep adding stripes. So the stripes remained at 13 to represent the original 13 states, and a star was added with each new state. Since 1959, when Hawaii and Alaska became states, the number of stars has remained at 50.

Materials

- construction paper
  background—white, 12" x 18" (30.5 x 45.5 cm)
  field—dark blue, 8" (20 cm) square
  stripes—red, slightly less than 1" x 18" (a little over 2 x 45.5 cm); 7 per student
- patterns for stars on page 85, reproduced on white construction paper
- scissors
- glue

Steps to Follow

1. Glue a red stripe along the top and bottom edges of the white paper.

2. Evenly space the 5 remaining red stripes and glue them down.

3. Glue the blue square to the upper-left corner of the flag.

4. Cut out the 13 stars and glue them in a circle on the blue square.

Star Patterns

Making Books with Pockets • January • EMC 584

Poor Richard's Almanack

Benjamin Franklin published *Poor Richard's Almanack* for 25 years. (He spelled the word almanac with a "k." In later years the "k" was dropped.) He sold about 10,000 copies each year. The "almanack" contained a calendar, holidays, weather forecasts, tide schedules, sunrise/sunset times, when to plant, advice, jokes, and poems.

Share *Ben Franklin's Poor Richard's Almanack for Kids*. This is a version of Benjamin Franklin's almanac that has been edited to be appropriate for children. Then have students create their own almanacs.

Materials

- almanac front and final page/back cover on page 84, reproduced on construction paper
- almanac pages 1 and 2 on page 85, reproduced on copier paper
- stapler
- scissors
- pencil

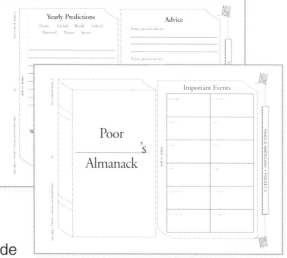

Steps to Follow

1. Front Cover—Have students write their own name on the cover. They can illustrate it with pictures of the seasons or a self-portrait.

2. Final Page/Back Cover—Important Events: List events and holidays for the upcoming year. Include holidays, birthdays, school events, etc.

3. Page 1—Advice: Students complete the sentence starters with personal advice.

4. Page 2—Yearly Predictions: Students make predictions of what will occur during the upcoming year. Predictions may be personal (home, school, friends) or general (national, world, sports, natural disasters). Students also draw or list weather predictions.

5. Additional Pages—Poor Richard's Almanac also included jokes and poems, as well as information about the tides, moon cycle, and sunrise/sunset. Cover the print on page 85 and reproduce blank pages if you wish your students to include additional material in their almanacs.

6. Cut out the pages and staple the book together.

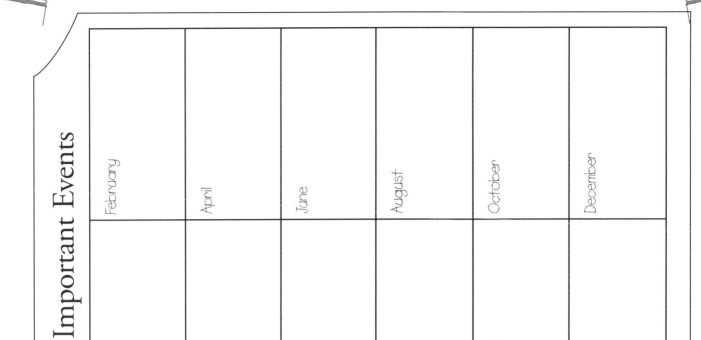

Important Events

February	January
April	March
June	May
August	July
October	September
December	November

staple or glue

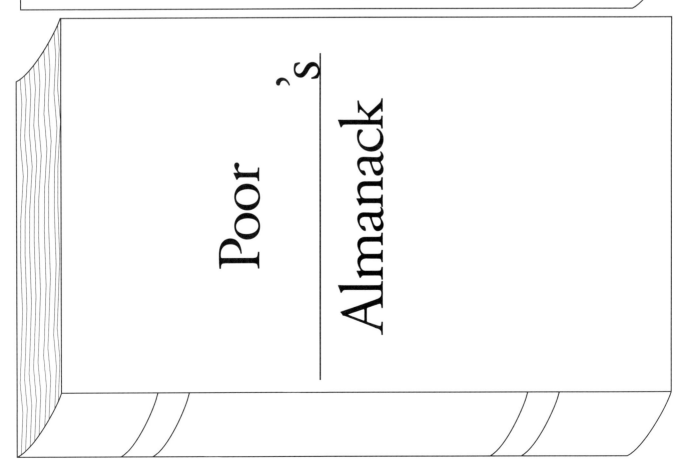

Poor ’s Almanack

Advice

A wise person always...

A wise person never...

A true friend...

A good neighbor...

Fish and visitors stink in three days.

staple or glue

Yearly Predictions

Home   Friends   World   School

National   Nature   Sports

Weather

spring

winter

summer

fall

staple or glue

Ben Franklin's Contributions

As your readings about Benjamin Franklin have probably related, his accomplishments were numerous and varied. Brainstorm with your students to recall things he did and things he invented or discovered.

This project will display a few of Franklin's contributions.

Materials

- construction paper
  kite—green, 12" x 18" (30.5 x 45.5 cm)
  kite "frame"—black, ¼" x 18" (1 x 45.5 cm) strips–2 per student
- patterns on page 87, reproduced on white construction paper
- glitter
- crayons
- glue
- 18" (45.5 cm) piece of yarn or roving
- fine-point black marking pen

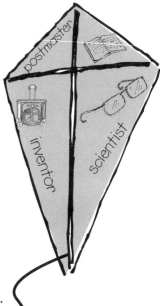

Steps to Follow

1. To make the kite shape, first fold the green paper in half lengthwise.

2. Hold the fold and cut as shown.

3. Glue one black strip down the center of the kite shape. Glue another black strip horizontally between the other two corners.

4. Color and cut out Ben Franklin's contributions (page 87).

5. Glue a picture in each of the four sections of the kite.

6. With a marking pen, label each picture: scientist (bifocals), inventor (stove), printer & author (book), postmaster general (letter).

7. Cut out the key. Put glue on the key and sprinkle on glitter.

8. When the glitter is dry, punch a hole at the bottom of the kite. Tie the yarn to both the kite and the key.

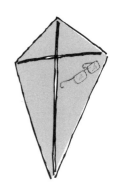

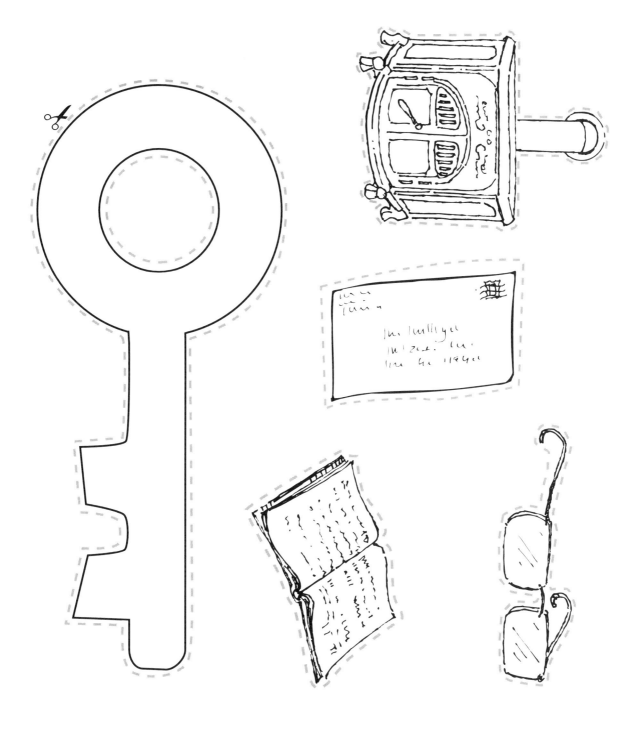

Dr. Martin Luther King, Jr.

Write about Dr. King

Share books and videos about this great contemporary American. As students tell what they remember, record their understandings on a chart. They can refer to the chart as they write.

Reproduce the writing form on page 89 for students to use. Set writing goals based on the abilities of your students.

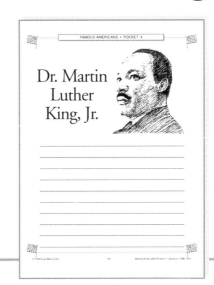

I Can Help

After learning about Dr. Martin Luther King, Jr.'s dream and his contributions to human rights, have students talk about what things they could do to make the world a better place for all people.

Materials

- hands pattern on page 90, reproduced on copier paper
- 4" x 18" (10 x 45.5 cm) construction paper (light-colored so that students can write on it)
- scissors
- pencils

Steps to Follow

1. Students color the hands to represent human skin and then cut them out.

2. Fold the construction paper in half crosswise and crease it lightly. Open the paper and fold each end to the middle and crease.

3. Put glue on the palms of the hands only. Attach to the flaps of the paper so that the fingers overlap or entwine.

4. Students open the hands and write one or more things that they can do to help the world be more like Dr. Martin Luther King, Jr.'s dream.

Dr. Martin Luther King, Jr.

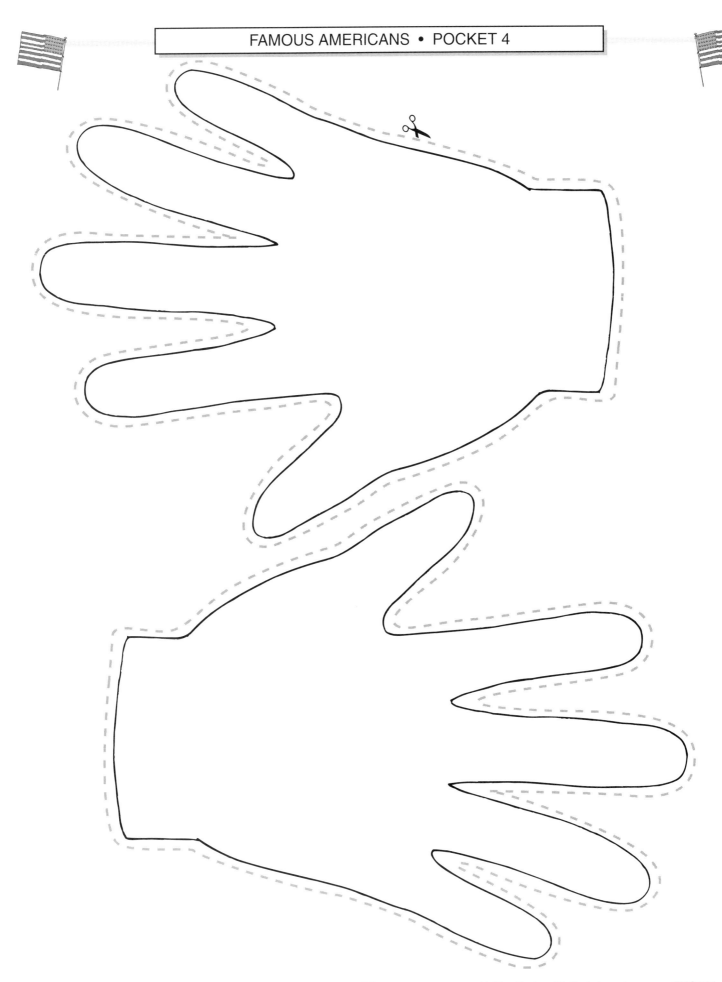

Note: Reproduce this page to label each of the four pockets of the Famous Americans book.

John Hancock

Pocket 1

Betsy Ross

Pocket 2

Benjamin Franklin

Pocket 3

Dr. Martin Luther King, Jr.

Pocket 4

kite

lightning bolt

Franklin stove

Benjamin Franklin

bifocal glasses

key

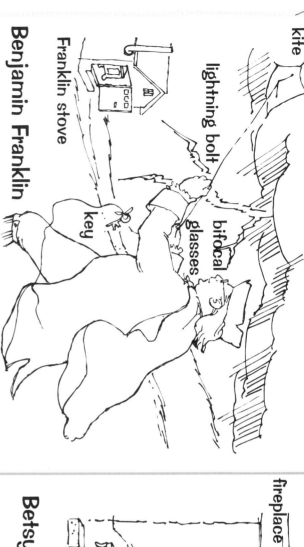

3-cornered hat

quill pen

breeches

Declaration of Independence

John Hancock

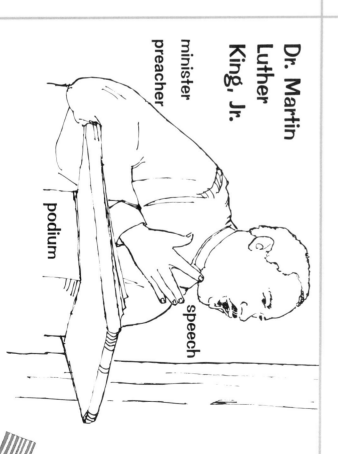

Betsy Ross

fireplace

sewing

flag

cap

Dr. Martin Luther King, Jr.

minister

preacher

podium

speech

Name: _____

Famous Americans

Bulletin Board Bonanza

Penguin Super Sentences—page 95

After the class has brainstormed words and phrases about penguins, this bulletin board becomes a center where students can write super sentences.

If you wish, these penguins can be a class art project as well. Choose four to decorate the bulletin board.

 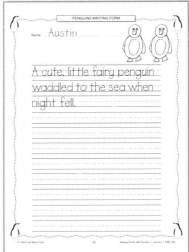

January Birthdays—page 96

A giant birthday cake helps to celebrate even more January birthdays. Involve your students in identifying people born in January.

Other January birthdays:

January 1	Paul Revere, 1735	January 24	Maria Tallchief, 1925
January 2	Isaac Asimov, 1920		Aaron Neville, 1941
January 3	Mel Gibson, 1956	January 26	Anita Baker, 1958
January 4	Louis Braille, 1809		Ellen DeGeneres, 1958
January 8	Elvis Presley, 1935	January 27	Lewis Carroll, 1832
January 17	James Earl Jones, 1931	January 29	Oprah Winfrey, 1954
January 19	Dolly Parton, 1946		

Penguin Super Sentences

Assemble four penguins and label them as shown. Tear the body, head, and stomach shapes. Add details cut from scraps of construction paper.

Descriptive Words

Kind of Penguin

Did What

Where or When

Cover the bulletin board as shown to represent the sea and ice.

On a table in front of the bulletin board, put containers, pencils, and copies of the penguin writing form.

Materials

- blue and white butcher paper
- construction paper
  penguin body—black, 9" x 12" (23 x 30.5 cm)
  penguin head—black, 6" (15 cm) square
  penguin tummy—white, 5" x 7" (13 x 18 cm)
  beak & feet—orange scraps
  eyes—black and white scraps
- black marking pen
- scissors
- glue

- stapler
- 4 cans, envelopes, or boxes
- strips of tagboard
- pencils
- penguin writing form on page 68

Write Super Sentences

1. Drawing on your study of penguins, brainstorm and list words and phrases in each of the four categories.

2. Write the words and phrases on tagboard strips and place them in the appropriate containers.

3. Route students through the writing center.

4. They are to pick one strip from each container to form a super sentence. Write one or more sentences on the writing form.

You've learned about four famous Americans with January birthdays. See how many other January people you can find—classmates, family members, sports and entertainment figures, authors, figures from history. This would make a good homework assignment.

Add a construction paper candle to the birthday cake for each January birthday. Write the person's name and the date of birth on the candle.

Make a giant birthday cake to fit your bulletin board. Decorate it with colorful stripes, polka dots, and "swooshes."

Materials

- colorful butcher paper
- construction paper
- scissors
- stapler
- marking pens

Make candles from appropriately sized strips of construction paper. Make plenty of candles to accommodate all the names students will find. Let students write the names and birthdays on the candles.